Planet
Protectors

THE INCREDIBLE
SMOG

BookLife
PUBLISHING

©2019
BookLife Publishing Ltd.
King's Lynn
Norfolk, PE30 4LS

All rights reserved.
Printed in Malaysia.

A catalogue record for this
book is available from the
British Library.

ISBN: 978-1-78637-651-0

Written by:
John Wood

Edited by:
Kirsty Holmes

Designed by:
Drue Rintoul

PHOTO CREDITS

All images are courtesy of Shutterstock.com. With thanks to Getty Images, Thinkstock Photo and iStockphoto. Front Cover – Egoreichenkov Evgenii, R-studio.
2 – VanderWolf Images. 4&5 – Stock_VectorSale. 6&7 – Multiverse, ribeiroantonio. 8&9 – Andrey Bayda, Kwangmoozaa. 10&11 – Amy Nichole Harris, Mary Terriberry.
12&13 – Tigergallery, Kit8.net. 14&15 – Pla2na, esbobeldijk. 16&17 – N-sky, Grimgram, Jemastock. 18&19 – Hung Chung Chih, Dragon Images. 20&21 – brown32.
22&23 – okawa somchai.

CONTENTS

Words that look like this can be found
in the glossary on page 24.

Time for a Mission

Ouch! That was a bad landing. My name is The Incredible Smog – you can just call me Smog. I am a Planet Protector and I need your help.

There are four Planet Protectors. We've looked after the environment since the beginning of time.

Look around you – the planet is dying! We're looking for someone to join our team and help us save it. Could it be you? Let's find out – we're going on a mission!

Our base is called Trashy Island. It is a fortress made out of recycled stuff.

There will be questions as you go through this book. Can you find the most eco-friendly answers and become a Planet Protector?

5

Getting Around

Things like cars, aeroplanes and factories create harmful gases. This is called air pollution. Harmful gases trap heat from the Sun in the Earth's atmosphere, and the planet gets hotter.

When the planet slowly gets warmer, it is known as climate change.

Damage Caused by a Hurricane

Climate change creates dangerous weather, such as hurricanes.

Climate change causes the sea ice in the North and South Poles to melt. This causes sea levels to rise, which leads to flooding.

Sea Ice

Come on, we need to get to the other side of the city. I can fly, but you will have to find your own way.

Question 1

Follow Smog!
How are you going to travel?

a) Private jet plane

b) Bicycle

c) Bus

At the end, your answers might earn you Planet Protector Points!

Making Electricity

A lot of our electricity is made by burning fossil fuels, such as coal and oil. Burning fossil fuels also creates harmful gases that hurt the planet.

This factory is burning coal and oil.

Air pollution can cause acid rain when it gets into the clouds. Acid rain can cause damage to things on land, especially animals that live in lakes and rivers.

Acid rain strips away the leaves from trees.

The Planet Protectors plan all their missions on their supercomputer at Trashy Island. It tells them where there is an environmental disaster!

An oil spill like this one is an environmental disaster. When oil gets into the sea, it harms the animals.

Question 2

Imagine you are on Trashy Island and it is time for a mission. What should you do with the supercomputer when you leave?

a) Put it on standby mode

b) Leave it running

c) Turn it off at the socket

Wind and Sun

There are ways of creating electricity that are friendly towards the environment, such as using wind turbines and solar panels. This is called renewable energy.

Wind Turbine

Solar Panel

Some houses have solar panels on their roofs.

Not only are fossil fuels harmful, but they will also run out one day. However, the Sun will always shine and the wind will always blow, which means we can use them forever.

15

Trashy Island uses solar panels. But look – one of the sheep has chewed through the wires! We've got no power!

Question 3

How are you going to get Trashy Island's electricity working again?

a) Use a backup source, such as a wind turbine

b) Burn some wood or coal to create power

c) Light a candle and wait for the repair person

Use It, Don't Lose It

Lots of things we need are made in factories, but factories create air pollution, and use a lot of electricity. In some cities, this is so bad that the people have to wear masks.

It's easy to use the same shopping bags every week, instead of buying new ones.

The more things we buy, the more things factories will make.
This means they will use more electricity and create more pollution.

The Planet Protectors are running low on **supplies**. We need to get some more.

AHH! SO MUCH LITTER!

Look, it's another Planet Protector — Super Binman! He's run out of litter pickers and bags.

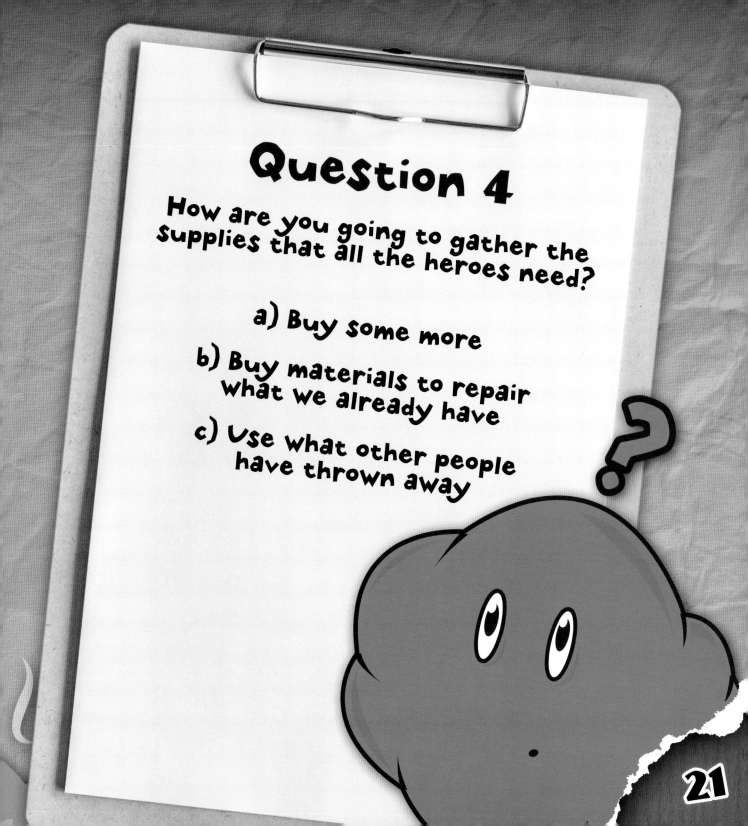

Question 4

How are you going to gather the supplies that all the heroes need?

a) Buy some more

b) Buy materials to repair what we already have

c) Use what other people have thrown away

A New Planet Protector?

It is time to add up your score. Here are the answers:

Question 1

A = 0 points

B = 2 points

C = 1 point

Question 2

A = 1 point

B = 0 points

C = 2 points

Question 3

A = 2 points

B = 0 points

C = 1 point

Question 4

A = 0 points

B = 1 point

C = 2 points

What did you get?

0–1
Oh no! You're an environmental disaster! Try again.

2–3
You've got a long way to go before you become a true Planet Protector.

4–5
You still have more to learn. Don't worry, you'll do better next time.

6–7
Not perfect, but you did very well. You would make a good side-kick.

8
Great score! You're our new Planet Protector! You start on Monday.

Glossary

atmosphere   the mixture of gases that make up the air and surround the Earth

electricity   energy used to power things

energy   the power required for an activity

environment   the natural world

fossil fuels   fuels, such as coal, oil and gas, which formed millions of years ago from the remains of animals and plants

gases   air-like substances that fill any space available

recycled   used again to make something else

supplies   useful things, such as money or materials

Index